THE
GUIDE
TO
BABY
SLEEP
POSITIONS

SURVIVAL TIPS FOR
CO-SLEEPING PARENTS

Andy He...
Co-cre...

D0973090

WARNING

The information in this book has not been tested, approved, or endorsed by experts of any kind, in any field. Consulting it may result in an increased or a decreased desire to have a baby, and on rare occasions may produce the condition referred to as "pee squirt" laughing. Not intended for parents lacking a sense of humor. NOT suitable for cleaning up diaper messes.

POTTER STYLE

www.crownpublishing.com | www.potterstyle.com | www.HowToBeADad.com

ISBN 978-0-449-81987-6

First Edition

PRINTED IN THE U.S.A.

Dear Reader,

This guide to baby sleep positions was compiled after extensive field research. We've spent our restless nights cataloging a baby's complete arsenal of sleep sabotage, including:

- BIOTERRORISM
  (see "The Exorcist" and "The Biohazard")

- ASSAULT AND BATTERY
  (see "The Mugging" and "The Roundhouse Kick")

- MIND GAMES
  (see "The Stalker" and "The Booby Trap")

This book is for those who are anticipating the torture and joy of co-sleeping, as well as veteran parents in need of the healing power of laughter. Consult the full-page diagrams for easy sleep-position identification. Check off the ones you've experienced or get a sneak-peek at the adventures ahead!

In Sleepless Solidarity,
Andy Herald and Charlie Capen

Like Father, Like Fetus

SUMMARY

Becoming a new parent is so nerve-racking that you may find yourself sleeping in the fetal position. You're about to enter an entirely new world, under extreme pressure, possibly kicking and screaming the whole way—not terribly unlike your baby. Don't worry, just think of this phase as an early way to relate to your child.

SIDE EFFECTS

- Rocking yourself gently
- Feeling extra cuddly
- Periodic fits of immaturity

TIPS

Cherish this position while it lasts; you definitely won't get to enjoy it as much once the baby arrives. And try not to worry too much. Good luck with that.

Difficulty:

Proficiency Level: ☐ Occurred ☐ In Progress ☐ Mastered

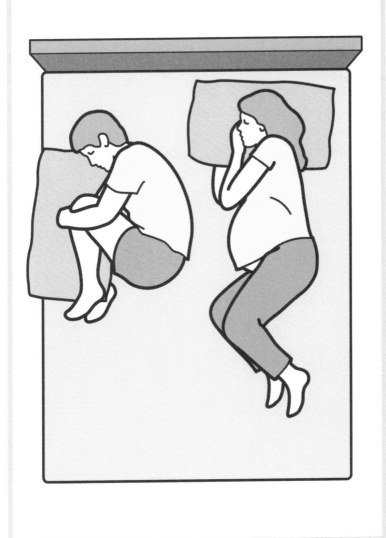

H Is for Hell

SUMMARY

Every parent knows this letter. Fears it! It's the *H*. Some may say it stands for "horrible" but don't listen to them; they're just whitewashing it. It stands for "Hell." And it's the kind of night you're both going to have.

SIDE EFFECTS

- Sleeplessness (applies to all sleep positions)
- Internal organ trauma
- Baby walks early

TIPS

You may want to do regular lower-back exercises, increase your medical coverage, or wear matching his-and-her Kevlar vests to bed. No matter how you position that baby, he will end up kicking or head-butting you in the back. Hard.

Difficulty:

Proficiency Level: ☐ Occurred ☐ In Progress ☐ Mastered

The Roundhouse Kick

SUMMARY

Co-sleeping can be special, or even necessary for some, but new parents don't usually realize that it can potentially lead to a broken nose, a fat lip, or an impressive black eye. It is possible to go to bed with a baby and wake up looking like you've been in a bar fight.

SIDE EFFECTS

- A lot of explaining to do the next day
- Development of catlike reflexes
- An impressive collection of ice packs

TIPS

Consider wearing a helmet with a face-shield to bed. It might not be comfortable, but at least the bags under your eyes won't be purple. And, remember, diapers and baby wipes are surprisingly effective for dealing with bloody noses.

Difficulty:

Proficiency Level: ☐ Occurred ☐ In Progress ☐ Mastered

The Petting Zoo

SUMMARY

Before you had a baby, it was probably cute as cookies when your pet climbed into bed with you. But now you've got the real deal, so it's time to establish a pecking order. They say, "two's company and three's a crowd," but four is a mosh pit. Sorry Fido and Whiskers, you're being evicted. Don't even think about barking or scratching on the door.

SIDE EFFECTS

- Accidentally petting the baby
- Guilty investment in pet toys
- Indoor pets become outdoor pets

TIPS

Eventually, your pets will get the picture, but if you have the resources, hire an animal psychologist to help with this transition.

Difficulty:

Proficiency Level: ☐ Occurred ☐ In Progress ☐ Mastered

The Spot Light

SUMMARY

What is that eyelid-prying laser beam of light? Is it the sudden glare of an oncoming vehicle? Nope. It's the bedside table lamp that your spouse has suddenly turned on at 2 a.m. You're stuck like a deer caught in the headlights, strapped in for another sleepless night.

SIDE EFFECTS

- Green spots in your vision
- Dreams of high-speed traffic
- Learning bedtime stories by heart

TIPS

Wear a sleep mask (bonus if you can find one lined with lead). Demand that spouse and baby listen to children's audio books with two sets of headphones or invest in parent- and child-sized night-vision goggles.

Difficulty:

Proficiency Level: ☐ Occurred ☐ In Progress ☐ Mastered

The Drive-Thru Window

SUMMARY

Being a baby is hungry business, day and night. All day. *All* night. So, expect repeated pit stops on the slumber highway. Obviously, the decision to bottle- or breastfeed will dictate whether dad gets to do his share of the driving. Happily for the baby, this is one drive-thru window where the order never gets screwed up.

SIDE EFFECTS

- Breast-revealing sleepwear takes on new meaning
- Arm falls asleep before baby does
- Never-ending advice from other parents

TIPS

If the baby pulls up to place a milk shake order with Dad, politely refer the customer to the next window. You'll be in your feeding position for a very long time. Get comfortable, or you'll feel like you were hit by a truck.

Difficulty:

Proficiency Level: ☐ Occurred ☐ In Progress ☐ Mastered

The Junkyard

SUMMARY

Most parents will fetch whatever it takes to put their kids to sleep. Don't judge them. You, too, will amass countless objects to pacify your little bundle of neediness. The end result is full-scale environmental destruction; in this case, the "environment" is the landfill that was once your bed. If you think stepping on a Lego block is painful, try sleeping on them.

SIDE EFFECTS

- Buyer's remorse
- Skin temporarily tattooed with toy shapes
- Hoarding

TIPS

If you can no longer find your bed, your baby, or both, call in a reality-TV crew or home-makeover show. The free clean-up compensates for the public shaming.

Difficulty:

Proficiency Level: ☐ Occurred ☐ In Progress ☐ Mastered

Donkey Kong

SUMMARY

Sleeping with your little one bouncing around in the bed can seem like a video game. In this case, Donkey Kong is metaphorically throwing barrels down at you as you try to ascend the steel girders of a good night's sleep. Unfortunately, even an endless supply of quarters won't help you master this parenting level.

SIDE EFFECTS

- Video game music stuck in your head
- Nightmares about barrels
- Desire to hit yourself with a hammer

TIPS

Cheat codes don't work here, and there is no online walk-through. Up, Down, Right, Left, Right, Left; learn to maneuver yourself into various positions without waking up the baby or your partner. Because if you do, it's Game Over.

Difficulty:

Proficiency Level: ☐ Occurred ☐ In Progress ☐ Mastered

The Pillow Thief

SUMMARY

Your little bundle of joy has stolen your pillow. You lay there and wrestle with a dilemma: Do you turn a blind eye and ride out the night without proper neck support? Or do you call the cops? Well, you can't really get mad, can you? That baby is just too cute. So, you choose to do the time for your little one's crime.

SIDE EFFECTS

- Numbness in "pillow arm"
- Impulse to dress baby in striped pajamas
- Parental martyrdom

TIPS

Steal one of your baby's largest stuffed animals. Turnabout is fair play, right? Sneak a secret pillow under your bed or in between your legs for later use.

Difficulty:

Proficiency Level: ☐ Occurred ☐ In Progress ☐ Mastered

The Hairdresser

SUMMARY

If babies could talk, they'd tell you how important style and hair care are for new parents. Sometimes your baby will play with your hair gently, which can be sweet and soothing. But since his motor skills can't be trusted, it is more likely that your "stylist" will end up jerking you awake with a good hard yank.

SIDE EFFECTS

- Hair falls out in clumps
- Dreadlocks
- Middle-of-the-night desire to shave your head

TIPS

Why not try to take advantage of the budding stylist in your bed? Squirt some leave-in conditioner in baby's little hands so that he can work on your snarls and split ends. You're welcome!

Difficulty:

Proficiency Level: ☐ Occurred ☐ In Progress ☐ Mastered

The Bat

SUMMARY

Bruce Wayne was probably a terrible sleeper and kept his ill-fated parents awake all night. This was probably his favorite position before he started running around in a cowl and cape. All babies seem to possess a batlike sonar for detecting their parents in the dark, which explains why you can't slip silently into a pitch-black room without waking baby up.

SIDE EFFECTS

- An unwelcome nocturnal lifestyle
- Feeling as if the life has been sucked out of you
- Baby could become a crime fighter

TIPS

If you're a fan of paranormal romance novels, you might start to suspect that you've given birth to a vampire. Check for fangs as your baby's incisors come in and take precautions!

Difficulty:

Proficiency Level: ☐ Occurred ☐ In Progress ☐ Mastered

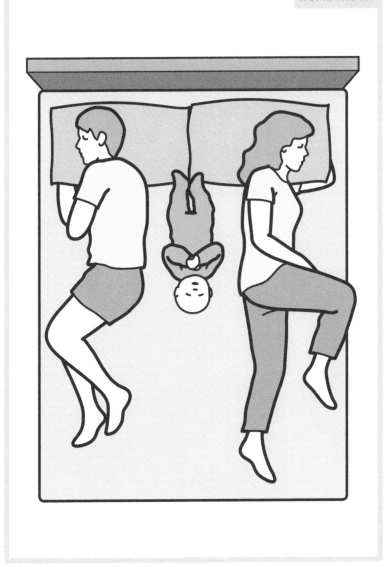

The Opera Singer

SUMMARY

The little sounds that a baby makes while sleeping are music to a parent's ears. Unless, of course, you are trying to get some shut-eye yourself. The never-ending bubbling sounds, the tiny squeaks and sighs, even an adorable little nose whistle can turn you into an unwilling insomniac. That's not to mention the scream-crying that can shatter wine glasses.

SIDE EFFECTS

- Temporary deafness
- Learning Italian
- Future *American Idol* contestant

TIPS

New parents tend to be on a hair trigger, ready to wake up at the drop of a pin. Thick pillows, sound machines, and earplugs have never been finer friends.

Difficulty:

Proficiency Level: ☐ Occurred ☐ In Progress ☐ Mastered

The Neck Scarf

SUMMARY

Small mammals are attracted to sources of warmth. This is especially true of baby humans, who don't have the advantage of thick fur coats or blubber. "The Neck Scarf" is, perhaps, your baby's way of placing herself over a warm pocket of air: *your mouth*.

SIDE EFFECTS

- Stiff neck
- Heat exhaustion
- Future world-champion professional wrestler

TIPS

Some babies love to be swaddled. "The Neck Scarf" might be your baby's way of returning the favor. Although it is tempting, your baby is not a suitable substitute for a heating pad, neck brace, scarf, or security blanket.

Difficulty:

Proficiency Level: ☐ Occurred ☐ In Progress ☐ Mastered

I'm Not Speaking to You

SUMMARY

If you've ever gone to bed after a spat, you know that territorial disputes and tugs-of-war over pillows and covers are commonplace. And now there is a baby on board, claiming at least one-third of the available real estate. Like an itty-bitty dictator, your child seizes control of the bedding, redefines the borders, and exiles you and your partner to the far corners of the bed.

SIDE EFFECTS

- Pouting in your sleep
- Martial law declared in bed
- Teeth chattering

TIPS

As you sulk in discomfort, you realize that there is extra incentive never to go to bed mad. Form an alliance with your partner to prevent sleepy-time tyranny from coming between the two of you.

Difficulty:

Proficiency Level: ☐ Occurred ☐ In Progress ☐ Mastered

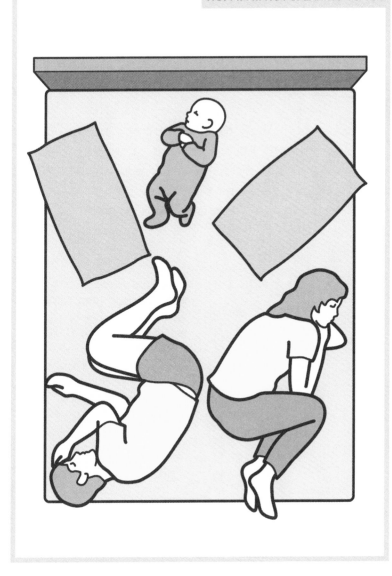

Roll-On Deodorant

SUMMARY

There is nothing better than the sweet powdery scent of a baby's head. Too bad it doesn't rub off on you after a night in this sleep position. Quite the opposite. In the morning, your young one will be coated in the ripe musk of new parenthood.

SIDE EFFECTS

- Baby hair loss
- Dulled "new baby" smell
- Animals avoid your baby

TIPS

If you have a newborn, there's a good chance that you're neglecting your own personal hygiene just a little bit. Try rubbing some delicious scents—like vanilla or rosemary—under your arms. If that doesn't work, strap on a couple of car deodorizers before hitting the hay.

Difficulty:

Proficiency Level: ☐ Occurred ☐ In Progress ☐ Mastered

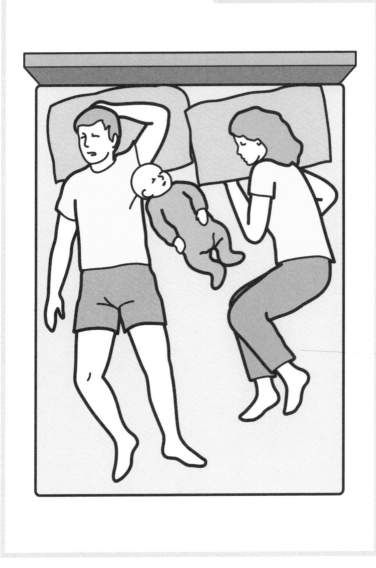

The Yin and Yang

SUMMARY

"Zen and the Art of Parenting" was the second choice for the title of this book, but alas, no Zen Masters were available, or harmed, in the creation of this guide. In this position, your little enlightened one is perched peacefully in the middle of two pillars of sleep-deprived suffering. Your bed represents a perfect balance between those who are asleep and those who are awake. Your baby is the former, and you are the latter.

SIDE EFFECTS

- Speaking in fortune-cookie phrases
- Peaceful baby (yes!)
- Moody, unenlightened parents (no!)

TIPS

Choose whether you are "the light end" or "the dark end" ahead of time. Fill your mind with emptiness; you're not capable of much else anyway. If all else fails, study feng shui.

Difficulty:

Proficiency Level: ☐ Occurred ☐ In Progress ☐ Mastered

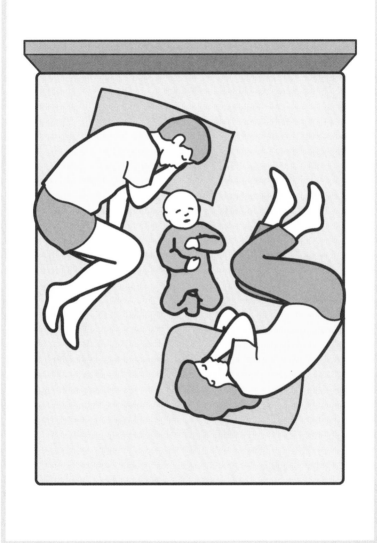

The Superman

SUMMARY

Most heroes are born from some great tragedy. In this scenario, the tragedy is your inability to sleep. It's nearly midnight, and your baby is faster than a falling bottle, more powerful than a choo-choo train, and able to leap tall building blocks in a single bound.

SIDE EFFECTS

- Awe of baby's stamina and strength
- Ability to drink tall coffees in a single gulp
- Child's future preference for tight underwear

TIPS

It's your duty to figure out what Kryptonite is keeping your baby from sleeping. A misplaced blanky (cape)? Does he need to replenish his super powers with a feeding? Did he soil his superhero suit?

Difficulty:

Proficiency Level: ☐ Occurred ☐ In Progress ☐ Mastered

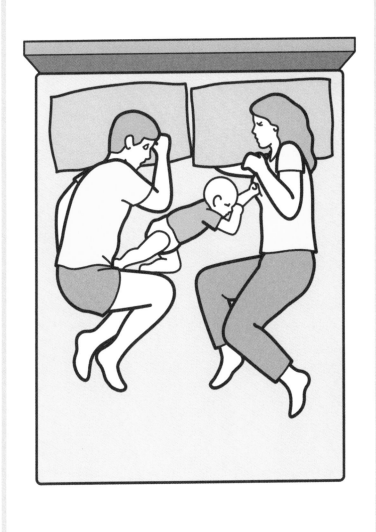

The Stalker

SUMMARY

Watching your adorable baby sleep is a pure Hallmark moment. But, when you open your eyes and catch your baby watching *you* sleep . . . it's more like a horror-movie moment. Even after confirming that blood is in fact *not* running down the walls, it's hard to shake this creepy feeling.

SIDE EFFECTS

- A sense that you're being watched
- Adult thumb sucking
- Fear of anything with unblinking eyes

TIPS

Whatever you do, don't break eye contact until baby blinks and gurgles reassuringly. All listed side effects are quadrupled if you find yourself in this position with multiple babies. Don't let them sense your fear.

Difficulty:

Proficiency Level: ☐ Occurred ☐ In Progress ☐ Mastered

Jazz Hands

SUMMARY

Some people nod off during musicals or plays, but when the off-Broadway performance is staged in your own bed, you'll find it hard to sleep through. Who knew that your baby was capable of Fred Astaire–level choreography? If you aren't a fan of tap dance and show tunes to begin with, your appreciation of jazz hands certainly won't improve at 3 a.m.

SIDE EFFECTS

- Unwanted back rubs
- The dreaded "Double Wake-Up"
- Future talent show winner

TIPS

Avoid exposing your baby to any talent-based reality shows. And remember, lulling your baby to sleep with music may increase the probability of a bedtime showstopper.

Difficulty:

Proficiency Level: ☐ Occurred ☐ In Progress ☐ Mastered

The Bungee Jumper

SUMMARY

You wake up and experience momentary heart failure because the baby isn't where you left her. You paw around the bed in the dark until your hand locates a chubby little leg. Relieved, you fall asleep again without releasing your gentle grasp. Your arm is now a safety line. Welcome to the extreme sport of parenting!

SIDE EFFECTS

- Awkwardly long handshake
- One arm becomes stronger than the other
- Never letting go—ever

TIPS

Fifteen minutes of vigorous stretching before bed will help prevent pulled muscles and other stress injuries, or purchase an elbow brace if you prefer buying stuff over exercising.

Difficulty:

Proficiency Level: ☐ Occurred ☐ In Progress ☐ Mastered

The Booby Trap

SUMMARY

You return to the dark bedroom after a nighttime bathroom expedition and sense that something's wrong. You peer into the shadows. It's a booby trap! Well, it's a baby trap at least. There is simply no way you can move the baby without waking her up. Indiana Jones had better odds replacing the golden idol with a bag of sand. And that didn't work out very well.

SIDE EFFECTS

- Shaky hands
- Holding your pee all night long
- Humming the *Mission Impossible* theme song

TIPS

Sleep on the floor or couch. Or treat the situation like a Band-Aid; remove your baby fast and be done with the suffering sooner. Next time, try saving your spot by leaving a jacket or bag in your place.

Difficulty:

Proficiency Level: ☐ Occurred ☐ In Progress ☐ Mastered

The Deflector Shield

SUMMARY

The space probe surges forward, requesting permission to land in the open docking bay of the waiting mother ship. Suddenly, a string of red-alert lights flash on the bedside monitor. WARNING! WARNING! A baby has created a dock blockade! Evasive maneuvers! The space probe veers off and powers down its engines, its payload undelivered.

SIDE EFFECTS

- Blue space balls
- A resentful mother ship
- Silence not unlike the vacuum of space

TIPS

To deactivate "The Deflector Shield": launch baby into arms of grandparent; book weekend trip to a galaxy far, far away; and lubricate mother ship with compliments, bubble baths, massages, and wine.

Difficulty:

Proficiency Level: ☐ Occurred ☐ In Progress ☐ Mastered

The Biohazard

SUMMARY

Where there's smoke there's fire, so when there's stink . . . you know the rest. A baby with a diaper at critical mass usually sounds the alarm by fidgeting or whining until one of you loses the who's-turn-is-it argument. On rare occasions, it's the smell that will hit you first. When your gag reflex actually wakes you up, you're looking at a true quarantine situation.

SIDE EFFECTS

- Random phantom whiffs
- Expertise handling of hazardous materials
- Shopping for new clothes

TIPS

Equip yourself with bleach, rubber gloves, and a Geiger counter. Burn all contaminated clothing and bedding immediately, and bury the evidence in the backyard before the authorities arrive.

Difficulty:

Proficiency Level: ☐ Occurred ☐ In Progress ☐ Mastered

The Dog House

SUMMARY

Every dad—actually, every *man*—knows this sleep position. It's "The Dog House." Before the baby, the couch was once a lonely island, a one-man leper colony for dudes in hot water. However, when there is a baby in your bed, the couch is more like a life raft—or even a weekend getaway! Both mother and father should take turns making reservations as often as possible.

SIDE EFFECTS

- Leg cramps
- Guilt (for actually sleeping)
- Upholstery marks on your face

TIPS

When shopping for a couch, test-drive all of the floor models for sleep comfort. Avoid hard-angled Danish modern furniture, but insist on drool-resistant fabric (a precaution for both you and the baby).

Difficulty:

Proficiency Level: ☐ Occurred ☐ In Progress ☐ Mastered

The Snow Angel

SUMMARY

Romping around in the snow can be a blast. Especially if you're a little ball of inexhaustible atomic energy. Actually, a baby doesn't even need snow; he is delighted to play in the fluffy drifts of your bedding. Right between the two of you. All night long.

SIDE EFFECTS

- Cravings for cocoa and mini marshmallows
- Worn-out sheets and blankets
- Drafty feeling in bed

TIPS

Practice clapping with your baby to wear out his arms before bedtime or encourage muscle fatigue by adding yoga weights to a favorite toy.

Difficulty:

Proficiency Level: ☐ Occurred ☐ In Progress ☐ Mastered

The Cow Tipper

SUMMARY

Being a parent is incredibly tiring, period. As a result, you'll rediscover a childlike ability to fall asleep anywhere, in any position. Sometimes even standing up. Be prepared to experience an entirely new definition of "falling" asleep. You'll wake up with rug burns on your face and carpet fibers in your teeth, which makes for an interesting story or status update.

SIDE EFFECTS

- Puddles of drool wherever you've clocked out
- Birds mistaking you for a statue
- Dreaming that you are falling (and it coming true)

TIPS

Construct a "corral" by placing pillows on the floor on your side of the bed to buffer your fall. Avoid loitering on pavement when exhausted. Seek further treatment at local coffeehouses.

Difficulty:

Proficiency Level: ☐ Occurred   ☐ In Progress   ☐ Mastered

The Mugging

SUMMARY

Waking up in sudden pain is very disorienting. Still half asleep, you peer around in the darkness, rubbing your latest injury. You take stock of your bedfellows; they are both sound asleep. Was it just a dream? The lingering pain and developing lump tell you it wasn't. You have no idea who hit you or with what, and you'll probably never know what actually happened. Maybe it was a ninja?

SIDE EFFECTS

- Sleeping with one eye open

- Random flinching throughout the night

- Fear of dark alleys and bedrooms

TIPS

Cover nighttime bottles in soft foam padding. Do not permit hard toys or stuffed animals with plastic eyes in bed. If the problem persists, set up a nanny cam for 24-hour surveillance.

Difficulty:

Proficiency Level: Occurred   In Progress   Mastered

The Exorcist

SUMMARY

Babies don't eat solid food, so they're pretty much locked and loaded for puke production. Baby vomiting doesn't necessarily mean a stomach virus or any illness at all. Sometimes it just happens spontaneously. Violently. Messily.

SIDE EFFECTS

- Fruit- or yogurt-scented hair
- Intimate knowledge of the digestive process
- Laundry. Lots of it.

TIPS

A baby can empty the entire contents of a full tum-tum in less than a second, so devise a quick cleanup plan. One of you hoses down the baby while the other strips and remakes the bed. Try completing this without completely waking up, so that the three of you can fall back asleep easily.

Difficulty:

Proficiency Level: ☐ Occurred ☐ In Progress ☐ Mastered

Forever Alone

SUMMARY

You've been fantasizing about the first night that your baby sleeps in his own bed. And then, that night arrives. It's just the two of you. You stare at the ceiling. You stare at each other. Like a lottery winner or someone just released from a long prison sentence, you just don't know what to do now.

SIDE EFFECTS

- Weeping uncontrollably
- Camping outside your baby's room
- Cradling your pillow like a baby

TIPS

You're gonna do it. Seriously, buy small baby-sized pillows you can hug. Make sure the route to your child's new bed is well illuminated so you don't stub your toes or bang your shins when you check on him, every night, repeatedly.

Difficulty:

Proficiency Level: ☐ Occurred ☐ In Progress ☐ Mastered

The Family Meeting

SUMMARY

You thought that co-sleeping was over and done with? Not so fast! An intense storm or a bad dream-palooza will bring children of all ages and sizes back into your bed. The wrestling, the noises, the jockeying for a place, the tangle of covers, ah yes, it's all very . . . cozy. You're all there together and that's what's important. Until you completely lose your mind.

SIDE EFFECTS

- "Alone time" becomes exchangeable currency
- Extra bodies raise temperature of room
- Desire to have another baby

TIPS

Depending on what you had for dinner, open the window a crack. Wait until the kids are asleep and relocate to less-crowded sleeping quarters. Cover your tracks by leaving a decoy pillow in your place.

Difficulty:

Proficiency Level: ☐ Occurred ☐ In Progress ☐ Mastered

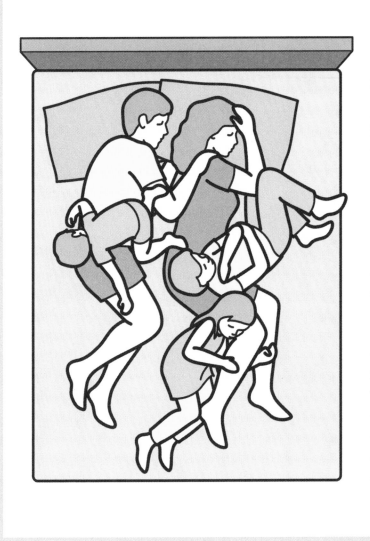

About Us

Andy and Charlie are cofounders and authors of HowtoBeaDad.com, an entertainment website for parents, non-parents, or anyone who's ever had parents, really. They're just two sleep-deprived friends with nothing left to lose but their sanity as they learn to be dads and try to look smart doing so.

If you're craving some industrial-sized drums of useless advice and humor about parenting, visit their website.

They're not experts, but that isn't gonna stop them from pretending. You've been warned.

Photo credit: Tami Bahat Photography*

* No preppy sweaters were harmed in the photographing of these subjects.

howtobeadad.com

Andy Herald

Charlie Capen